SAMSON: A TYPE OF CHRIST

BY BRIAN JOHNSTON

Copyright Hayes Press 2015

Published by:

HAYES PRESS Publisher, Resources & Media,

The Barn, Flaxlands

Royal Wootton Bassett

Swindon, SN4 8DY

United Kingdom

www.hayespress.org

---

1. http://www.Lockman.org

Table of Contents

CHAPTER ONE: ONE BORN REMARKABLY

———

Although we may tend to think of Samson primarily as a tarnished hero; in some ways he can be viewed as prefiguring Christ. That's the approach we want to take in this book which will focus on the life of Samson. From Judges chapter 13, the parallels begin with the news that Samson the saviour is born. Yes, he, too, was a saviour – so at his birth a saviour was born. In fact, as soon as his parents were told of his arrival in advance, they were also told what his mission would be: "he shall begin to deliver Israel from the hands of the Philistines" (v.5).

Deliverance from oppressing enemies was once again the need of the hour due to the depressing fact that "the sons of Israel again did what was evil in the sight of the LORD, so that the LORD gave them into the hands of the Philistines for forty years." We say depressing because this has already become an all too familiar pattern in the book of Judges, at least for anyone who's read it through thus far. What we find recorded is a repeating cycle of Israel falling away from their obedience to the LORD, then the LORD's judgement of them at the hand of their enemies, and then yet another story of the LORD delivering his people when at last they cry out to him for help.

Although, having said that, there's a difference this time round. More precisely, there's something missing, something we've come to expect. There's no mention about Israel "crying out" to the LORD in this time of distress (cf. 3:9, 15; 4:3; 6:6-7; 10:10). Perhaps their cry had often been a cry for help in trouble, rather than a serious confession of sin. But even so, on this occasion, even that kind of cry is missing. Well, having noticed this, surely it's worth registering the point that if God's help were given to us only when we prayed for it, and actually asked for it – if God's help was given to us only when we had sense enough to seek it, how much worse off we would be!

But let's get back to the story of Samson. I want to share with you the first 3 verses of Judges chapter 13. When you read, remember the point we've just made about them not crying out to the Lord for help, and then notice what we're told about the woman who is to become the saviour's mother:

> "Now the sons of Israel again did evil in the sight of the LORD, so that the LORD gave them into the hands of the Philistines forty years. There was a certain man of Zorah, of the family of the Danites, whose name was Manoah; and his wife was barren and had borne no children. Then the angel of the LORD appeared to the woman and said to her, "Behold now, you are barren and have borne no children, but you shall conceive and give birth to a son. (Judges 13:1-3)

So, yes, the next thing we meet that's different in the story of this particular deliverer is that the mother-to-be, the wife of Manoah is barren. The heavenly messenger, who's described as the Angel of the LORD even seems to rub it in with his first words to her: "you are barren; and have borne no children" (v. 3). But then immediately she begins to hear wonderful words like "shall conceive," "birth," and "son." They formed part of God's plan for her life which was now being shared with her: "you shall ... give birth to a son; and no razor shall come upon his head, for the boy shall be a Nazirite to God from the womb; and he shall begin to deliver Israel from the hand of the Philistines" (v.5).

I think there are at least six or seven barren women featured in the Bible. Abraham's wife, Sarah, agonized over her barrenness (Genesis 11:30–21:1). Rebekah's first twenty years of marriage were childless (Genesis 25:19-26). Rachel was both barren and resentful until she at last bore Joseph (Genesis 29:31–30:24). Then after the time of Samson, we meet Hannah (1 Samuel 1) and then in the New Testament, Elizabeth (Luke 1). (There was also the unnamed, but notable, woman of Shunem). The curious fact is that all the sons who were the products of the longings of these women tend to prefigure Christ in a rather striking way – but I'm afraid we don't have time to go into that now, it'll have to be something for your own personal follow up.

Here, in Judges 13, the woman – Samson's mother-to-be, is both barren and anonymous. We don't even know her name. She is Manoah's wife and becomes Samson's mother, but her name's not given to us. To her sterility the Bible has added obscurity. Maybe, there's another lesson right there for us too. The story of salvation becomes a reality for each one of us when we discover that it's not about us: we're no good; and can do nothing about it ourselves. We need a saviour whom God alone can provide – and that saviour is Jesus Christ.

But wait, as we draw parallels between Samson and Jesus, let's first think again about how the news of Samson's birth was brought to Manoah and his wife: "The angel of the LORD appeared to the woman and said to her, "... you are barren and have borne no children, but you shall conceive and give birth to a son." (Judges 13:3)

If we're in the business of tracing parallels between Samson and Jesus – which we are doing in this study - then this is a very obvious one. For news of Jesus' birth was also heralded by a heavenly messenger, as we read in Luke's Gospel, chapter 1:

> "Now ... the angel Gabriel was sent from God to a city in Galilee called Nazareth, to a virgin engaged to a man whose name was Joseph, of the descendants of David; and the virgin's name was Mary. And coming in, he said to her, "Greetings, favored one! The Lord is with you." But she was very perplexed at this statement, and kept pondering what kind of salutation this was. The angel said to her, "Do not be afraid, Mary; for you have found favor with God. And behold, you will conceive in your womb and bear a son, and you shall name Him Jesus." (Luke 1:26-31)

And like Manoah, Joseph also received a similar visitation, as Matthew tells us:

"Now the birth of Jesus Christ was as follows: when His mother Mary had been betrothed to Joseph, before they came together she was found to be with child by the Holy Spirit. And Joseph her husband, being a righteous man and not wanting to disgrace her, planned to send her away secretly. But when he had considered this, behold, an angel of the Lord appeared to him in a dream, saying, "Joseph, son of David, do not be afraid to take Mary as your wife; for the Child who has been conceived in her is of the Holy Spirit. She will bear a Son; and you shall call His name Jesus, for He will save His people from their sins." (Matthew 1:18-21)

It's that last part of the angel's message that's so similar to the message brought from heaven to announce the fact that Samson was soon to be born: "he shall begin to deliver Israel from the hands of the Philistines" (v. 5). Now, most of Judges chapter 13 is Samson's nativity story, and it concentrates on the circumstances of his birth. Just two verses contain all we know of Samson's childhood, and this is what they tell us:

"Then the woman gave birth to a son and named him Samson; and the child grew up and the LORD blessed him. And the Spirit of the LORD began to stir him in Mahaneh-dan, between Zorah and Eshtaol." (Judges 13:24-25)

These are only the only two sentences we have which relate in any way to Samson's childhood. Obviously, the writer isn't interested in giving us a full biography or he wouldn't have omitted all the details of Samson's childhood. And clearly he thinks Samson's birth story is very important or he wouldn't have devoted such attention to it.

When we compare the New Testament, we find the details we're given about Jesus follow the same pattern. Both Matthew and Luke devote significant space to Jesus' ancestors, birth, and infancy and, certainly, to his public ministry. But we have virtually nothing about his childhood except the mention of his visit to the temple as a boy of 12 (Luke 2:41-52). Finally, we remind ourselves that Judges 13, where we hear of Samson's nativity story, ends with a mention of the Holy Spirit's involvement in his life:

> "And the Spirit of the LORD began to stir him in Mahaneh-dan, between Zorah and Eshtaol" (Judges 13:25). Again, this is reminiscent of the early record of our Lord's life, about whom Luke says: "Jesus, full of the Holy Spirit, returned from the Jordan and was led around by the Spirit in the wilderness." (Luke 4:1)

May the Holy Spirit who was active in their lives, be active in ours too. He will, if we allow him. And may we know his help as we study God's Word together. Christ gave us encouragement to look for himself in all the Scriptures, so let's keep looking for ways in which Samson was meant to prefigure Christ, the ultimate saviour. Naturally, there're many contrasts as time and again Samson failed. But I invite you to join me in majoring on the positive – all the positive ways we can see a foreshadowing of the Lord Jesus Christ in the events of Samson's life.

CHAPTER TWO: THE NAZIRITE

The story of Samson is one which has perhaps had more than its fair share of exposure at the hands of film directors and song-writers. And the reason is obvious enough. The story line provides scope for imaginative embellishments featuring a flawed hero as male lead with the kind of love interest that appeals so much to Hollywood. Christ, however, gave us encouragement to look for himself in all the Scriptures, and so our approach in this study is to look for ways in which Samson was meant to prefigure Christ, the ultimate saviour.

Having considered in the last chapter the circumstances of his birth, we now come to the fact that he was to be a Nazirite – that's someone under a special vow of dedication to God. The terms and conditions of this vow were spelled out in the third book of Moses, the Old Testament book of Numbers. The fact that Samson was to be a Nazirite must be important because it's repeated several times in the early part of his story (ch.13 vv.7,13,14).

We should remind ourselves of how the news of Samson's special life of dedication was broken to his parents to be, along with the news of his impending birth. Here are the words spoken to his mother:

"Now therefore, be careful not to drink wine or strong drink, nor eat any unclean thing. For behold, you shall conceive and give birth to a son, and no razor shall come upon his head, for the boy shall be a Nazirite to God from the womb; and he shall begin to deliver Israel from the hands of the Philistines." Then the woman came and told her husband, saying, "A man of God came to me and his appearance was like the appearance of the angel of God, very awesome. And I did not ask him where he came from, nor did he tell me his name. But he said to me, 'Behold, you shall conceive and give birth to a son, and now you shall not drink wine or strong drink nor eat any unclean thing, for the boy shall be a Nazirite to God from the womb to the day of his death.'"

Then Manoah entreated the LORD and said, "O Lord, please let the man of God whom You have sent come to us again that he may teach us what to do for the boy who is to be born. God listened to the voice of Manoah; and the angel of God came again to the woman as she was sitting in the field, but Manoah her husband was not with her. So the woman ran quickly and told her husband, "Behold, the man who came the other day has appeared to me." Then Manoah arose and followed his wife, and when he came to the man he said to him, "Are you the man who spoke to the woman?" And he said, "I am." Manoah said, "Now when your words come to pass, what shall be the boy's mode of life and his vocation?"

So the angel of the LORD said to Manoah, "Let the woman pay attention to all that I said. She should not eat anything that comes from the vine nor drink wine or strong drink, nor eat any unclean thing; let her observe all that I commanded." (Judges 13:4-14)

As we said, the Nazirite vow, which Samson was to follow, is fully described in the Bible book of Numbers, chapter 6. Generally speaking, the Nazirite vow was voluntary and temporary. Not so with Samson. In his case, the vow was to be in force from the womb to the tomb – so, in terms of the extent of his dedication, he reminds us of the lifelong dedication of Samuel and John the Baptist. In fact, Samson's period of abstinence – as a Nazirite - even began in the womb before his birth, due to his mother being commanded not to eat grape products. There were 3 main requirements for such a vow as the one Samson lived under, the details of which are given in Numbers chapter 6. First we're told that:

"When a man or woman makes a special vow, the vow of a Nazirite, to dedicate himself to the LORD, "he shall abstain from wine and strong drink; he shall drink no vinegar, whether made from wine or strong drink, nor shall he drink any grape juice nor eat fresh or dried grapes. All the days of his separation he shall not eat anything that is produced by the grape vine, from the seeds even to the skin." (Numbers 6:3-4)

This abstinence from grape products obviously prevented the individual who was so dedicated from being affected by the harmful effects of indulging in strong drink. But this abstinence from wine must surely further symbolize alertness and sobriety – things which we mention because they're enjoined on all of us who would claim to be followers of Christ. Take First Thessalonians chapter 5 verse 6, where Paul says: "so then let us not sleep as others do, but let us be alert and sober." So, as far as we're concerned today, alertness and sobriety are basic requirements of living a consecrated life in dedicated service for the Lord – although not necessarily in our case meaning total abstinence from all alcohol. We must, however, be very careful and moderate with its use.

So, abstinence from grape products was the first requirement, to which was added a second: 'All the days of his vow of separation no razor shall pass over his head. He shall be holy until the days are fulfilled for which he separated himself to the LORD; he shall let the locks of hair on his head grow long. (Numbers 6:5)

Long, uncut hair was to become the obvious sign of the Nazirite's total commitment and subjection to God. Samson's great strength was not somehow magically produced by his long hair, of course. We need to be clear that the secret of his strength lay in God by means of Samson remaining faithful to his vow – and that faithfulness was symbolized by his uncut hair. It's interesting that in First Corinthians chapter 11, the apostle Paul, in verse 14, cites nature as teaching us that if a man has long hair then it's a dishonour to him.

Certainly, then, a man with a Nazirite vow was not seeking his own honour, but was focusing on living for the honour of God. He denied himself, while living as one who was committed to a higher 'law'. We, too, are to be 'living sacrifices' (Romans 12:1), living for the Lord Jesus who died and rose again that we should live not for ourselves, but for him who so loved us (2 Corinthians 5:15). Denying ourselves, we are to follow Christ (Luke 9:23). And finally, there was a third requirement:

> "All the days of his separation to the LORD he shall not go near to a dead person. He shall not make himself unclean for his father or for his mother, for his brother or for his sister, when they die, because his separation to God is on his head. All the days of his separation he is holy to the LORD. (Numbers 6:6-8)

It seems clear that this emphasis on the avoidance of contact with dead bodies was intended to signify holiness and purity. What was a ceremonial requirement then, is now a spiritual condition in our lives of service for the Lord. As we read in the New Testament: "For this is the will of God, your sanctification" (1 Thessalonians 4:3). And with that the apostle John agrees, saying: "We will see Him just as He is. And everyone who has this hope fixed on Him purifies himself, just as He is pure" (1 John 3:2b-3).

Now as we look for ways in which Samson was a picture of our Lord Jesus Christ, we're naturally led to think of Christ as the ultimate example of someone whose entire life was wholly dedicated to God. It's true that our Lord was not technically a Nazirite: he drank wine and reached out to raise the dead, but he was the one who could say in John chapter 17:19: "For their sakes I sanctify [or consecrate] Myself, that they themselves also may be sanctified [or set apart] in truth."

Our Lord's whole life was devoted to the one object of glorifying God and doing his will. And the Lord's lifelong dedication in separation to the will of God took him to the cross of Calvary, and included in the great purpose for which he died, was the objective that we should also be positively separated to God in truth – and not only as individuals, but marked out as a separated people.

Something I noticed some little while ago, and quite enjoyed, so I'll share it with you, is this: that when in those days of the Old Testament, a Nazirite came to the end of the period of his vow of consecration, he had to offer a sacrifice, a peace offering. But this was no ordinary sacrifice or peace offering, for in this case, the Lord, or at least his representative, the priest, got something extra – you'll have to look up the details in Numbers chapter 6 (vv.19,20) – but it's just that thought of how the Lord gets more from lives that are dedicated in his service – that should be a real incentive to us when we think about it.

Now, one last point if I may. There's something exceptional here in the instruction given to Samson's mother, which we read earlier. She was also, quite unusually, to be bound by the requirement to avoid grape products. It was necessary, of course, to ensure Samson was a Nazirite even from the womb, from before his birth. But here's the practical point for us, especially if we're Christian parents: does it not point up the value of the prayerful and careful example of parents in bringing up children? More things are caught than are taught ...

CHAPTER THREE:
OVERCOMING THE LION

In this study of Samson, we're looking at some ways in which it's possible for us to see Samson as prefiguring Christ. In this chapter, let's think of him as the one who overcame the lion. Let me remind you, from Judges chapter 14, of the incident in which Samson encountered the lion in question:

> "Then Samson went down to Timnah and saw a woman in Timnah, one of the daughters of the Philistines. So he came back and told his father and mother ... Then Samson went down to Timnah with his father and mother, and came as far as the vineyards of Timnah; and behold, a young lion came roaring toward him. The Spirit of the LORD came upon him mightily, so that he tore him as one tears a young goat though he had nothing in his hand; but he did not tell his father or mother what he had done." (Judges 14:1-6)

We notice that it was with his bare hands – and in the Spirit's power – that Samson defeated the lion. Now we might possibly associate that detail from the life of Samson with the Bible's teaching that we simply cannot overcome the Devil in our own strength. For you may remember that one of the ways in which the Bible describes the Devil is as a roaring lion. And that's how we entered upon this train of thought: for the lion came roaring towards Samson. In fact, it's the apostle Peter who warns us to: "Be of sober spirit, be on the alert. Your adversary, the devil, prowls around like a roaring lion, seeking someone to devour" (1 Peter 5:8).

But, in a sense, we digress by bringing ourselves into the picture. The point of our study is primarily to look from Samson to the Lord Jesus. Let's do that now, but stay with the point of the Lord overcoming the Devil, just as Samson overcame the roaring lion. As a bridge back from ourselves to the Lord, we remind ourselves that in the Garden of Eden, the Devil showed himself to be more than a match in knowledge and power for humanity in the form of our first parents. So, if the Devil was to be defeated, it wasn't going to be by us. And the apostle John confirms this was the reason for the Lord coming into the world: it was to 'destroy the works of the devil' (1 John 3:8). In all his life on earth, the Lord Jesus was victorious over the Devil. And in death, he rendered him powerless (Hebrews 2:14).

Now let's aim to learn lessons from the Lord, who, like Samson, defeated the lion. Remember what it says in Luke chapter 4:

> "Jesus, full of the Holy Spirit, returned from the Jordan and was led around by the Spirit in the wilderness for forty days, being tempted by the devil. And He ate nothing during those days, and when they had ended, He became hungry. And the devil said to Him, "If You are the Son of God, tell this stone to become bread." And Jesus answered him, "It is written, 'MAN SHALL NOT LIVE ON BREAD ALONE.'" (Luke 4:1-4)

Christ's 'weapon' in overcoming the Devil's temptations was his use of the 'sword of the Spirit', which is the Bible (Ephesians 6:17). But don't think you can ward off the Devil's attacks simply by quoting any Bible verses you know. Our Lord lived in the Scriptures. His ways were ordered by God's Word; it was in his heart, and so his lip was consistent with his life. That was the power behind what he said that day.

Perhaps, we can contrast this with Samson. For, as we read over the record, there's little or no indication of any enjoyment or use of Scripture in his life. Perhaps this was the strongman's weakness. With the Lord, by contrast, we find the verses of the Old Testament frequently on his lips. This clearly indicates that he delighted in and meditated on the Law of God, like the blessed man of Psalm 1. What we've just read from Luke chapter 4 about the Lord's temptation by the Devil demonstrates what we're saying.

Let's be clear. The Devil knew very well who the Lord was. So instead of translating the temptation as "If You are the Son of God, tell this stone to become bread", it would be better - and quite legitimate – to translate it as "Since you are the Son of God, tell this stone to become bread". The Devil was not asking the Lord to prove his identity. Not at all - even the demons knew that; but he was tempting the Lord to misuse the very power and authority which truly belonged to him as the Son of God. The Lord had been fasting for 40 days, what was the harm in asking him to do something he was well capable of doing, simply in order to satisfy his hunger? Was that not a legitimate thing to do?

No, not when it meant going outside of the will of God, his Father – who gave him all the works he had to do. They were the Father's works, not the Lord's own (John 14:10). And the Lord never performed any miracle for his own benefit. Bread - or food - is necessary to satisfy our physical needs, but the Lord's answer to the Devil clearly demonstrates a deeper level of satisfaction that was always present in the life of Jesus Christ.

The Lord's words were a quotation from Israel's desert experience as they journeyed to the Promised Land – a Bible section he must have meditated upon here in his time in the desert: his understanding proving its relevance in every age. The Lord practised, in those 40 days of fasting in the desert, the truth Israel hadn't learned in the whole 40 years of their desert experience; namely that there's a deeper level of sustenance to be found – and it's found in that which proceeds from the mouth of God.

The words of God's mouth, the God-breathed scriptures, were Jesus' constant delight. Our Lord overcame the roaring lion not just by simply quoting Scripture at him, but because he lived every day in the reality and the power of God's Word. Doing the will of God as revealed in Scripture was his true meat and drink. And if the Word of God is our primary source of satisfaction, if we allow it to truly sustain us, then the Tempter's tactics against us will be far less effective.

Well, that was all from reading about Samson overcoming the roaring lion by the Spirit of the Lord, and with nothing in his hand - but showing it was in the power of God alone. But if only Samson had found his primary source of satisfaction in God's Word! Then his God-given strength would always have been directed according to God's will. But there's more that catches our attention in this story-line. Let's find out what happened next to Samson:

> "So he went down and talked to the woman; and she looked good to Samson. When he returned later to take her, he turned aside to look at the carcass of the lion; and behold, a swarm of bees and honey were in the body of the lion. So he scraped the honey into his hands and went on, eating as he went. When he came to his father and mother, he gave some to them and they ate it; but he did not tell them that he had scraped the honey out of the body of the lion."
> (Judges 14:7-9)

Even here, perhaps there's a hint of Samson's carelessness in the things that matter to God. Down by the vineyards - of all places - Samson's drawn back to the carcase of the lion. Finding honey there, he scraped it out and ate it, sharing it with his parents – but not disclosing where it had come from. By looking to Samson, we find ourselves drawn here once again to the person of the Lord Jesus. Jesus was victorious in life over the Devil, and over all his temptations. And by dying on the cross in the will of God, Jesus has broken the power of the Devil - who although he does still roar against us, is ultimately a defeated adversary. The Lord overcame the lion, and shares the sweetness of his triumph with us. We're superbly blessed, through believing, for our debt of sin is cancelled. But what a blessing that the Lord also breaks the power of cancelled sin! And even that's just the beginning!

What the cross of Jesus has achieved remains hidden from many, as things unheard of and unimaginable. Listen to the apostle Paul in First Corinthians chapter 2:

> "... but we speak God's wisdom in a mystery, the hidden wisdom which God predestined before the ages to our glory; the wisdom which none of the rulers of this age has understood; for if they had understood it they would not have crucified the Lord of glory; but just as it is written, "Things which eye has not seen and ear has not heard, and which have not entered the heart of man, all that god has prepared for those who love him." For to us God revealed them through the Spirit; for the Spirit searches all things, even the depths of God." (1 Corinthians 2:7-10)

In the life of every true believer lives the Spirit of God. By his Spirit, God reveals to us now the depth of blessings that are ours for all eternity. That is, they're ours if we believe on the Lord Jesus. They're only for those in a relationship with him – those who have obeyed the Word of God (Luke 8:21). You remember how only Samson's parents enjoyed with him the sweetness of the honey which came from the defeated lion. The joy of the blessings Christ has won for us remains inexplicable to non-believers, but their sweetness is reserved for all those who are related to Christ by their faith in him – he, who as the true deliverer, came to deliver his people from their sins and to destroy the works of the Devil and to share the sweetness of eternal blessings with all those related to him by the obedience of their faith.

CHAPTER FOUR: LONE FIGHTER

———

S amson was a judge, and a man of tremendous strength – a kind of Hebrew Hercules if you like! He hated the Philistines who'd been troubling Israel for 40 years (Judges 13:1), and was prepared to fight them single-handed. He seems, at times, to have been motivated by little more than personal vengeance, yet in the New Testament he's named among the heroes of faith (Hebrews 11:32). In some ways he's an enigma to us. The picture which emerges of him is of someone who fought with his wits as well as with his fists. These features are illustrated in the next episode from the life of Samson. It's set at the time when Samson was to be married to his Philistine bride, and we read:

> "Then his father went down to the woman; and Samson made a feast there, for the young men customarily did this. When they saw him, they brought thirty companions to be with him. Then Samson said to them, "Let me now propound a riddle to you; if you will indeed tell it to me within the seven days of the feast, and find it out, then I will give you thirty linen wraps and thirty changes of clothes. "But if you are unable to tell me, then you shall give me thirty linen wraps and thirty changes of clothes." And they said to him, "Propound your riddle, that we may hear it."

So he said to them, "Out of the eater came something to eat, And out of the strong came something sweet." But they could not tell the riddle in three days. Then it came about on the fourth day that they said to Samson's wife, "Entice your husband, so that he will tell us the riddle, or we will burn you and your father's house with fire. Have you invited us to impoverish us? Is this not so?" Samson's wife wept before him and said, "You only hate me, and you do not love me; you have propounded a riddle to the sons of my people, and have not told it to me." And he said to her, "Behold, I have not told it to my father or mother; so should I tell you?"

However she wept before him seven days while their feast lasted. And on the seventh day he told her because she pressed him so hard. She then told the riddle to the sons of her people. So the men of the city said to him on the seventh day before the sun went down, "What is sweeter than honey? And what is stronger than a lion?" And he said to them, "If you had not plowed with my heifer, You would not have found out my riddle." Then the Spirit of the LORD came upon him mightily, and he went down to Ashkelon and killed thirty of them and took their spoil and gave the changes of clothes to those who told the riddle. And his anger burned, and he went up to his father's house. But Samson's wife was given to his companion who had been his friend." (Judges 14:10-20)

It may at first seem tempting to draw a connection between Samson's riddle and the parables of the Lord, or at least with the Lord's questions which so perplexed his unbelieving audiences – questions like 'if the Christ is David's son why then does David call him 'Lord'?' (Mark 12:35). And 'What was the source of the baptism of John, from heaven or from men?' (Matthew 21:25). But any comparison like that would surely be quite superficial.

What's more interesting at this stage of the story is how we begin to discover how Samson was to operate in his work of beginning to deliver the Israelites from their Philistine oppressors. For we read he went out against them as a lone warrior. This is a big difference between Samson and other earlier judges who raised armies. If Samson isn't unique in this respect, at least he's an outstanding example of a judge or deliverer who fought single-handedly. Samson stood alone, without helpers, in his work of deliverance. It seems the Israelites didn't rally around him.

Samson didn't raise an army, nor did the Israelites even follow his lead and pursue their enemies when Samson had them on the back foot. In this way, our attention is drawn to the Lord. As the hymn says: 'In the fight, He stood alone.' No-one could share in the work of deliverance which the Lord Jesus had come both to begin and to finish. His own people hadn't received him, and at the end, even his disciples deserted him. 'There was none other good enough to pay the price of sin'. It had to be the work of the Saviour alone.

The Lord Jesus Christ must die on Calvary, bearing sin, and die utterly alone as the sin-bearer. That was one battle that only he could fight. He alone had to suffer and bleed and die - for our waywardness, our wilfulness. It was there on the cross he paid the price of our rebellion. But Samson's own wilfulness, it appears, led him into single-handed action against Israel's national enemy, the Philistines. Notice the sequel where we'll find Samson once again taking solo action. Remember where we've already got to in the story of Samson. He's married a Philistine woman (of Timnah). This forbidden alliance, strangely enough, was 'of the Lord' (Judges 14:3) who 'sought an occasion against the Philistines'. Under pressure, Samson's new wife has schemed to betray his confidence, at which Samson has taken revenge on the Philistines, killing 30 of them. Then Samson left her and returned home. What happened next is as follows:

> "... after a while, in the time of wheat harvest, Samson visited his wife with a young goat, and said, "I will go in to my wife in her room." But her father did not let him enter. Her father said, "I really thought that you hated her intensely; so I gave her to your companion. Is not her younger sister more beautiful than she? Please let her be yours instead." Samson then said to them, "This time I shall be blameless in regard to the Philistines when I do them harm." Samson went and caught three hundred foxes, and took torches, and turned the foxes tail to tail and put one torch in the middle between two tails.

When he had set fire to the torches, he released the foxes into the standing grain of the Philistines, thus burning up both the shocks and the standing grain, along with the vineyards and groves. Then the Philistines said, "Who did this?" And they said, "Samson, the son-in-law of the Timnite, because he took his wife and gave her to his companion." So the Philistines came up and burned her and her father with fire. Samson said to them, "Since you act like this, I will surely take revenge on you, but after that I will quit." He struck them ruthlessly with a great slaughter; and he went down and lived in the cleft of the rock of Etam." (Judges 15:1-8)

It seems Samson was unaware that his bride had been given by her father to his friend, possibly his best man, and so he went back later to visit her. Discovering what had happened, he took even greater revenge on the Philistines by destroying their crops. When they then retaliated and killed his wife, Samson defeated them yet again – this time with a great slaughter.

If Samson was often, if not primarily, motivated by personal revenge – as this example seems to show – then that's a major contrast with Christ, who prayed for his enemies. Remember …

"When they came to the place called The Skull, there they crucified Him and the criminals, one on the right and the other on the left. But Jesus was saying, "Father, forgive them; for they do not know what they are doing." And they cast lots, dividing up His garments among themselves" (Luke 23:33-34).

Previously, Jesus had pronounced forgiveness himself – as in the case of the paralyzed man. On that occasion, recorded in Mark's gospel, chapter 2, he'd said to the paralytic, "Son, your sins are forgiven" (v.5). But now, here on the cross, he prays to his Father in heaven to forgive them. Why the difference? Is it because here at the cross, Jesus, though still the Son of God, was now our representative, identifying with us so that he might, in the will of God, die the just for the unjust that he might bring us to God (1 Peter 3:18)?

But how wonderful that he was not crying out for vengeance upon those who so wrongfully abused him! There's one reference in the Bible to the blood of Christ which describes it as 'speak[ing] better than the blood of Abel' (Hebrews 12:24). That refers us back to early human history and the story of Cain and Abel. To a time when Cain had just killed his own brother because his brother's sacrifice had been accepted by God, while Cain's own offering had not. Now God speaks to Cain:

> "Then the LORD said to Cain, "Where is Abel your brother?" And he said, "I do not know. Am I my brother's keeper?" He said, "What have you done? The voice of your brother's blood is crying to Me from the ground." (Genesis 4:9-10)

It's usually thought that Abel's spilt blood was crying out from the ground for vengeance. But, we're told, the blood of Christ speaks better than that of Abel. The blood of Christ's cross doesn't cry out for vengeance. Instead, it speaks peace to all who trust in his death for our sins. How wonderful! – the blood of

Christ calls for pardon on the guilty. Have you received that pardon, forgiveness from the only one who – all alone – could deliver us from our sins?

CHAPTER FIVE: BETRAYED AND THIRSTING

———

The point we've reached in the story of Samson is the point where he's taken revenge on the Philistines for bringing about the death of his wife and father-in-law. It says of Samson that he struck the Philistines ruthlessly with a great slaughter, and then he went and lived in the cleft of the rock of Etam. Obviously, it was only a matter of time before they were going to come after him - which is exactly what happened, as we read in Judges chapter 15:

> "Then the Philistines went up and camped in Judah, and spread out in Lehi. The men of Judah said, "Why have you come up against us?" And they said, "We have come up to bind Samson in order to do to him as he did to us." Then 3,000 men of Judah went down to the cleft of the rock of Etam and said to Samson, "Do you not know that the Philistines are rulers over us? What then is this that you have done to us?" And he said to them, "As they did to me, so I have done to them."
>
> They said to him, "We have come down to bind you so that we may give you into the hands of the Philistines." And Samson said to them, "Swear to me that you will not kill me." So they said to him, "No, but we will bind you fast and give you into their

hands; yet surely we will not kill you." Then they
bound him with two new ropes and brought him up
from the rock." (Judges 15:9-13)

Now, in this study, we've been looking out for things which
happened to Samson which are similar in some way to what
happened to the Lord Jesus, the ultimate deliverer. We've just
read of Samson being betrayed by his own people. Naturally, our
thoughts turn to Judas betraying the Lord. Our Lord's betrayal at
the hands of Judas Iscariot was in fulfillment of Psalm 55, which
said:

"For it is not an enemy who reproaches me, Then I
could bear it; Nor is it one who hates me who has
exalted himself against me ... But it is you ... My
companion and my familiar friend; We who had
sweet fellowship together." (Psalm 55:12-14)

Matthew's Gospel, in chapter 26, explains what happened to
Jesus:

"Then one of the twelve, named Judas Iscariot, went
to the chief priests and said, "What are you willing to
give me to betray Him to you?" And they weighed out
thirty pieces of silver to him." (Matthew 26:14-15)

And so later:

"Judas, one of the twelve, came up accompanied by a
large crowd with swords and clubs, who came from
the chief priests and elders of the people. "Now he

who was betraying Him gave them a sign, saying, "Whomever I kiss, He is the one; seize Him." Immediately Judas went to Jesus and said, "Hail, Rabbi!" and kissed Him. And Jesus said to him, "Friend, do what you have come for." Then they came and laid hands on Jesus and seized Him." (Matthew 26:48-50)

And so, as the hymn says, 'they bound the hands of Jesus in the garden where he prayed ... and led him through the streets in shame'. With that picture of a man being led away bound, let's return to Samson now, as the men of Judah lead him to the Philistines. Like Jesus, Samson is also bound, but ...

"When he came to Lehi, the Philistines shouted as they met him. And the Spirit of the LORD came upon him mightily so that the ropes that were on his arms were as flax that is burned with fire, and his bonds dropped from his hands. He found a fresh jawbone of a donkey, so he reached out and took it and killed a thousand men with it. Then Samson said, "With the jawbone of a donkey, Heaps upon heaps, With the jawbone of a donkey I have killed a thousand men." When he had finished speaking, he threw the jawbone from his hand; and he named that place Ramath-lehi. Then he became very thirsty ..." (Judges 15:14-18)

It seems Samson felt he was dying of thirst. Some see in this threat of death and subsequent revival, a reflection of Jesus' death and resurrection. But, there's another way of looking at it, perhaps one which is more closely related to the story-line ...For in his victory song at first, Samson doesn't appear to give God the glory, does he? He sings his own praises, recording his mighty achievement in his own words: "With the jawbone of a donkey, Heaps upon heaps, With the jawbone of a donkey I have killed a thousand men." It seems to be all about what Samson has done. Was that why, I wonder, God humbled him with thirst? Then, fearing he was going to die of thirst, Samson now says: "You have given this great deliverance by the hand of Your servant, and now shall I die of thirst and fall into the hands of the uncircumcised?"

That's quite a change of perspective. Samson has now realized, or at least acknowledged, that the victory he'd known that day was actually God's victory through him: he said to God, 'you have given this great deliverance.' That's a vital lesson we can learn along with Samson here. For it's not what we do for God; but it's what we allow him to do through us.

Some of us will remember President Kennedy's words to the American people: "Don't think about what America can do for you; but about what you can do for America." The message for us might be: 'Don't think about what God can do for you; but about what you can ... allow God to do through you' – notice, it's not even what we can do for God; but what we can allow him to do through us. This is the lesson Samson had to learn.

Jesus himself – having become man to be our Saviour – Jesus always demonstrated the principle that Samson had to learn here. Jesus worked in complete dependence on his Father. Giving thanks was often the expression of that dependence. For example, in John chapter 6, it says: Jesus 'gave thanks' – that's the unusual and remarkable way in which the miraculous feeding of the 5,000 is characterized (verse 23). To give thanks in this way is to express grateful confidence in someone else's ability. Having given thanks, Jesus' own part in that wonderful miracle was simply to act on the assumption that God, his Father, would work. The miracles were not so much evidence of what Jesus himself could do, but evidence of what the Father was doing through him. Indeed, they're described as 'miracles, wonders and signs, which God did among you through him' (Acts 2:22).

Faced with the circumstances of a hungry crowd and only 5 loaves and two small fish, Philip saw only the impossibility of the situation they were in. Two hundred days' wages wouldn't provide enough bread to feed all the crowd which had gathered. While Andrew saw only the inadequacy of the available resources: a mere five barley loaves and two fish. But in the same circumstances, Jesus was focused – with gratitude - on the sufficiency of his Father. That's why this simple statement of Jesus' 'giving thanks' is so impressive. And we're to learn from it: "Whatever you do in word or deed, do all in the name of the Lord Jesus, giving thanks through Him to God the Father' (Colossians 3:17). And also: 'in everything give thanks; for this is God's will for you in Christ Jesus" (1 Thessalonians 5:18).

In every situation, especially those bigger than our ability and resources, we're to do as Jesus did, which is to express a disposition of grateful dependence, and then act. It's not giving thanks for adversity; it's giving thanks for the opportunity to prove that God is sufficient to meet the need - it's having the confidence to know that he's able. That "it is God who is at work in you, both to will and to work for His good pleasure"

(Philippians 2:13). God calls us to a task – just like he called Samson to be a deliverer – so he calls us too: not that we might do it for him; no, for the Bible reminds us: "He who calls you is faithful; he will surely do it" (1 Thessalonians 5:24 ESV). God calls us that we might become the means through which he himself does it – through us.

Well, that's what we've learnt, or perhaps, re-learnt, through Samson's thirst, but we should finish the story of how God satisfied Samson's thirst:

> "God split the hollow place that is in Lehi so that water came out of it. When he drank, his strength returned and he revived. Therefore he named it En-hakkore, which is in Lehi to this day." (Judges 15:19)

En-hakkore means the fountain of the one who called. Notice it was found here at Lehi (Lechi) which means 'jaw' or 'jawbone': the place where Samson used the jawbone of an ass to such devastating effect. I hardly think it's possible for us to piece all this together and not to be drawn in our thoughts to another skull hill – the one where Christ died, known as 'Calvary'. It was there, upon the cross, that our saviour called out 'I thirst' (John 19:28). He thirsted then, having borne our sin in his body on the tree, so that we might never have thirst in our souls for all eternity. Yes, there's lasting refreshment – for those who call upon Jesus Christ as their personal saviour, having turned from their sins, and turned to him in faith.

It's at the end of this chapter that we read: "So he judged Israel twenty years in the days of the Philistines" (Judges 15:20) That seems premature, for usually that's the form the epitaph takes on the life of a judge like Samson. Maybe it's where the story should've ended – in victory, with a picture of Christ, the ultimate Saviour. Chapter 16 is a sad episode in personal failure for Samson – something which spoils the picture, but more of that in the next chapter ...

CHAPTER SIX: ONE WHO COULD NOT BE HELD CAPTIVE

———

In March 2007, a documentary called The Lost Tomb of Jesus, drew more than 4 million viewers when it aired on the Discovery Channel. It claimed an ancient family tomb, unearthed in 1980 during the construction of a Jerusalem apartment complex, once held the bones of Jesus' family, including his mother, Mary, his "son" (Judah) and Mary Magdalene, supposedly Jesus' wife.

A companion book, "The Jesus Family Tomb," quickly rocketed to sixth place on The New York Times nonfiction best-seller list. The film and book suggest that a first-century stone box found in a south Jerusalem cave in 1980 contained the remains of Jesus, contradicting the Christian belief that he was resurrected and ascended to heaven. This belongs to the same genre of religious fiction recently found to be so lucrative by Dan Brown of the Da Vinci Code notoriety.

Of course, such claims as we've mentioned are a total contradiction of Bible-believing Christianity. The film created a firestorm of worldwide attention, but the documentary received criticism and negative reviews from professing Christians and atheists alike. David Mevorah, curator of the Israel Museum, writing in the New York Times, said: "Suggesting that this tomb was the tomb of the family of Jesus is a far-fetched suggestion".

While Jodi Magness, an archaeologist at the University of North Carolina, said in the Washington Post: "This whole case [for Jesus' tomb] is flawed from beginning to end".

> Well, how does this issue relate in any way, shape or form to the story of Samson which we're following in this series? We've been highlighting the contrasts and comparisons we can make between Samson and Jesus Christ, the ultimate saviour. As we now begin to look at Judges chapter 16, it's first of all a contrast that's immediately obvious ...

> "Now Samson went to Gaza and saw a harlot there, and went in to her. When it was told to the Gazites, saying, "Samson has come here," they surrounded the place and lay in wait for him all night at the gate of the city. And they kept silent all night, saying, "Let us wait until the morning light, then we will kill him.""

Perhaps we're reminded of how the psalmist sometimes spoke of his enemies prowling around at night waiting their opportunity to strike (Psalms 55:10; 63:6-9). But for various people in the Bible, God's deliverance came at midnight (e.g. Exodus 12:29; Acts 16:25), and it was the same here, for we read on that ...

> "Now Samson lay until midnight, and at midnight he arose and took hold of the doors of the city gate and the two posts and pulled them up along with the bars; then he put them on his shoulders and carried them up to the top of the mountain which is opposite Hebron." (Judges 16:1-3)

Now, what I'm reminded of is the hymn which says:

'Vainly they watch His bed,

Jesus, my Saviour!

Vainly they deal the dead,

Jesus, my Lord!

Death cannot keep its prey,

Jesus, my Saviour!

He tore the bars away!

Jesus, my Lord!' (Lowry)

Yes, the resurrection of Jesus! In Acts 2:24 we read that it was impossible for him to be held in death's power. He burst forth, like Samson from the city of Gaza. All the futile efforts that'd been made to guard his body were shown to be useless. The fact of Jesus' historical and bodily resurrection is the complete answer to all the religious fiction of the Da Vinci Code and the Lost Tomb. I was interested to read the words of British journalist Mark Tully. He'd been revisiting the scene of Jesus' life to interview people for a BBC TV series on Jesus. He ended with his own view in which he said: '[Jesus] taught in strange riddles. He didn't convince his fellow Jews. And he didn't overthrow Rome. From that failure I have come to what, for me, is the most important conclusion of all. That the hardest ... article of

Christian faith, the resurrection, must have happened. If there had been no miracle after Jesus' death, there would've been no grounds for faith ... No resurrection ... no church.'

But since you may still be wondering if it really can be true, let's try to imagine what all the other possibilities are. Perhaps the first idea that occurs to you is that: 'hey, may be Jesus never actually died in the first place'. Could it be that in the cool of the tomb he revived? Well that would mean that the execution crew of Roman soldiers that day, with the centurion in charge of them, somehow got it wrong. But they wouldn't have dared to leave anything to chance, not in this politically charged case. They were experienced professionals, they knew their job well, grim though it was. Although they didn't feel the need to break Jesus' legs - so sure were they that he was already well and truly dead - they did certify him dead by thrusting a spear into his side and drawing blood and water in a separated mass: the evidence of death.

Next, Joseph of Arimathea took charge of the burial in typical Jewish fashion. After the body was washed, it was wrapped foot to head in linen grave clothes. Then, because it was the custom, what they did was apply aloe and myrrh - a kind of gooey tree resin. In this way the grave-clothes were in a very real sense glued on the body. With the spices, these grave-clothes weighed as much as a hundred pounds (John 19:39)! And then, of course, there was the small matter of a two-ton stone rolled against the mouth of the rock-hewn tomb, which the authorities then had sealed and guarded with soldiers. With so many people that day wanting him dead and buried, and with all the precautions that were taken, first to establish death, and then to secure the tomb itself, it's simply beyond belief that Jesus somehow revived and escaped.

Okay then, someone might say: 'But isn't it possible that the followers of Jesus who reported the empty tomb on the third day, the women folk, actually went to the wrong tomb - after all, they were in a state of shock? They went to a different tomb by mistake and it so happened that that tomb was empty.' Think about it - how could anyone mistake the tomb of someone who was really important to them, especially when that tomb had been sealed and further identified by having an armed guard posted at it! In any case, they recognised the grave-clothes lying just as they'd left them in the now empty tomb.

Suppose the body was stolen then. Let's check that possibility out. Well, if the culprits were supposed to be Jesus' disciples, then they'd first have needed to overpower the guards. The authorities had taken effective measures against exactly this kind of thing being attempted. But even if you were to persist in thinking this might still have happened, what we would then have to believe is that the disciples would later be martyred for something that they knew full well was a lie, a hoax. Someone might well die for something false - if they sincerely believe it to be true. But that's not the situation here. What we're having to suppose in this theory is that the very people who fabricated the evidence gave their lives defending their own made-up lie - not very realistic I'm sure you'll agree.

And if it was either the Jews or the Romans who'd contrived the disappearance of the body of Jesus, then at any time afterwards, they could've killed off this annoying new, upstart religion by simply producing the body and parading it down the main street of Jerusalem. But what possible motive would they have for stealing the body in the first place? There again you might say it was all in the mind of these early disciples. It was mere wish-fulfilment, or perhaps it was an illusion - you know those alleged appearances of Jesus in resurrection. After all, there are some weird enough stories around today that someone somewhere knows someone who thinks they saw Elvis on some porch in Hawaii.

Doesn't fit the evidence either. The disciples don't seem to have had the remotest thought of any such thing as resurrection, despite the fact Jesus had given them clues earlier. After the shock of Jesus' being taken and crucified, they were in disarray and depression. Without any prospect of anything beyond, they went through with performing the full Jewish burial ritual. Yes, they really expected then that Jesus was going to stay dead. When the news of his resurrection broke and he began to appear to them, they were slow to leave their state of disbelief. Nor were Jesus' resurrection appearances fleeting, isolated visions claimed only to have been seen by a few.

No, within a few weeks hundreds of people had seen him alive. But you know what the most significant thing of all for me is? It's the transformation that took place in the lives of his previously demoralized followers. They had experienced the power of Christ's resurrection - he who 'when he ascended on high ... led captive a host of captives, and he gave gifts to men' (Ephesians

4:8; Psalm 68:18, note v.27). These very words too seem like a far greater echo of still more words from that epic battle-song of long ago: 'Arise, Barak, and take away your captives, O son of Abinoam' (Judges 5:12). And, what's more, the Gates of Hades shall not even prevail against his Church! The Lord, like Samson, truly did tear the bars away!

.

CHAPTER SEVEN: ONE WHO WAS TEMPTED

———

A Swiss lady once advertised for a chauffeur and received three job applications. She interviewed them individually, each time asking the same question: "How close to a precipice could you drive and still be safe?" The first assured her that he could come within 15 centimeters in complete safety. The second applicant boasted that he could let his outer wheel run on the edge and still have nothing to worry about. The third and last candidate admitted that he didn't know, but that he'd simply prefer to keep as far away as possible. Needless to say, he got the job! In those terms, Samson was someone who drove too close to the edge of temptation. The result was he went over the edge. Judges chapter 6 tells us how it happened:

> "After this it came about that he loved a woman in the valley of Sorek, whose name was Delilah. The lords of the Philistines came up to her and said to her, "Entice him, and see where his great strength lies and how we may overpower him that we may bind him to afflict him. Then we will each give you eleven hundred pieces of silver." So Delilah said to Samson, "Please tell me where your great strength is and how you may be bound to afflict you." Samson said to her, "If they bind me with seven fresh cords that have not been dried, then I will become weak and be like any other man."

Then the lords of the Philistines brought up to her seven fresh cords that had not been dried, and she bound him with them. Now she had men lying in wait in an inner room. And she said to him, "The Philistines are upon you, Samson!" But he snapped the cords as a string of tow snaps when it touches fire. So his strength was not discovered. Then Delilah said to Samson, "Behold, you have deceived me and told me lies; now please tell me how you may be bound." He said to her, "If they bind me tightly with new ropes which have not been used, then I will become weak and be like any other man."

So Delilah took new ropes and bound him with them and said to him, "The Philistines are upon you, Samson!" For the men were lying in wait in the inner room. But he snapped the ropes from his arms like a thread. Then Delilah said to Samson, "Up to now you have deceived me and told me lies; tell me how you may be bound." And he said to her, "If you weave the seven locks of my hair with the web and fasten it with a pin, then I will become weak and be like any other man."

So while he slept, Delilah took the seven locks of his hair and wove them into the web]. And she fastened it with the pin and said to him, "The Philistines are upon you, Samson!" But he awoke from his sleep and pulled out the pin of the loom and the web. Then she said to him, "How can you say, 'I love you,' when your heart is not with me? You have deceived me these three times and have not told me where your great strength is."

It came about when she pressed him daily with her words and urged him, that his soul was annoyed to death. So he told her all that was in his heart and said to her, "A razor has never come on my head, for I have been a Nazirite to God from my mother's womb. If I am shaved, then my strength will leave me and I will become weak and be like any other man." When Delilah saw that he had told her all that was in his heart, she sent and called the lords of the Philistines, saying, "Come up once more, for he has told me all that is in his heart." Then the lords of the Philistines came up to her and brought the money in their hands.

She made him sleep on her knees, and called for a man and had him shave off the seven locks of his hair. Then she began to afflict him, and his strength left him. She said, "The Philistines are upon you, Samson!" And he awoke from his sleep and said, "I will go out as at other times and shake myself free." But he did not know that the LORD had departed from him. Then the Philistines seized him and gouged out his eyes; and they brought him down to Gaza and bound him with bronze chains, and he was a grinder in the prison" (Judges 16:4-20).

What a disaster! And it all seems so unnecessary. But Satan knows where each of us is weak. As Samson began to make reference to his hair, he was beginning to get very close to the edge – and to toy with the serious matter of his consecration. We need to take this as a warning, as we look now to the Lord in setting for us by contrast the perfect example in overcoming temptation. In Luke 4:3-12 we read:

> "... the devil said to Him, "If you are the Son of God, tell this stone to become bread." and Jesus answered him, "it is written, 'man shall not live on bread alone.'" And he led him up and showed him all the kingdoms of the world in a moment of time. And the devil said to him, "I will give you all this domain and its glory; for it has been handed over to me, and I give it to whomever I wish. "Therefore if you worship before me, it shall all be Yours." Jesus answered him, "It is written, 'You shall worship the Lord your God and serve him only.'" And he led him to Jerusalem and had him stand on the pinnacle of the temple, and said to him, "If you are the Son of God, throw yourself down from here; for it is written, 'He will command his angels concerning you to guard you,' and, 'On their hands they will bear you up, so that you will not strike your foot against a stone.'" And Jesus answered and said to him, "It is said, 'You shall not put the Lord your God to the test.'" (Luke 4:3-12)

The Lord had been fasting for 40 days. Was it not a legitimate thing to satisfy his hunger? Not when it meant going outside of the will of God, his Father. Bread - or food - is necessary to satisfy our physical needs, but the Lord's answer to the Devil clearly demonstrates a deeper level of satisfaction that was always present in the life of Jesus Christ. The Lord's words were a quotation from Israel's desert experience as they journeyed to the Promised Land, words pointing to a deeper level of sustenance to be found in that which proceeds from the mouth of God. The words of God's mouth, the God-breathed Scriptures, were Jesus' constant delight. Our Lord overcame not by simply quoting Scripture, but because he lived every day in the reality and the power of the Word of God. Doing the will of God as revealed in Scripture was his true meat and drink. And if the Word of God is our primary source of satisfaction, if we allow it to truly sustain us, then the Tempter's tactics against us will be far less effective.

Satan next promised the Lord the world and all its glory, if he would but fall down and worship him. Some think of this as Satan merely offering the Lord a short-cut to what would one day quite legitimately be his – so that the nature of the temptation lay in the fact that it was a tempting offer to by-pass the cross of suffering. Others take the view that this tempting offer consisted of something wrong in itself: something worldly was on offer: it was all about self-glorifying power. Well, perhaps, there's a reconciling view: namely, that at the time of Satan's offer, with the world lying in the evil one, there was a decidedly negative aspect to what was on offer; whereas, in the future when the kingdom of this world has become the kingdom of the Lord and his Christ (Revelation 11:15), the world and all its glory will rightly belong to Christ in the will of God.

Now, the word for worship in this exchange between Satan and Jesus basically means submission. Submission to Satan was the price Satan demanded here for gaining the world. And not only here, but we see it again in Revelation chapter 14 - where worshiping the beast (or antichrist) is the condition for gaining acceptance within the end-time world-system - even at the most basic level of being able to buy and sell. The apostle John confirms that the world lies in the evil one, as Satan's own words to the Lord implied. And so, the person set upon worldly gain, the person who desires advancement in the things of this world – will of necessity have submitted already to the authority of the one in whose control these things lie.

It may seem somewhat stark to equate a lifestyle of worldly advancement with submitting to, or actually worshiping, the Devil, but the two main words for worship in the New Testament are used by Jesus in his rejection of Satan's tempting offer. What this appears to highlight is that worship in its widest sense embraces the totality of our lifestyle choice. What we submit to, and what we devote our time and energy to by serving it or pursuing it – that's the thing, or the one, we're worshiping. The Lord triumphed over temptation because of his total submission to the Father whom he served with devoted service. What an example and lesson for us!

And still there's a third victory by our Lord over temptation which we can learn from. Satan tempted the Lord to throw himself down from the pinnacle of the temple so as to put God's promise in scripture to the test: that the angels would bear him up. The Lord's answer was ready: we're not to put God to the test like that. It's enough to stand steadfastly on the promises, having a sincere faith in the Word of God. If we don't doubt God's Word, but simply have faith to take him at his Word, we'll be preserved from falling into many a temptation.

So, it's been by way of total contrast that we've looked away from Samson to our Lord Jesus – and seen how in this matter of overcoming temptation, there's no substitute for sustenance and satisfaction from the Word; submission and service in worship; and steadfastness in our walk, not doubting the promises of God. The Lord was tempted in all points as we are, but – unlike Samson – he was without sin! (Hebrews 4:15).

CHAPTER EIGHT: ATTAINING HIS GREATEST VICTORY IN DEATH

W e now come to the last chapter in Samson's life. Foolishly, he's allowed himself to be tempted and betrayed by a woman he thought loved him. But she revealed the secret of his strength to his Philistine enemies. Samson had toyed with his consecration, and the symbol of that consecration, his uncut hair, had been removed and with it went his strength, for we read that the Lord had left him.

> "However, the hair of his head began to grow again after it was shaved off. Now the lords of the Philistines assembled to offer a great sacrifice to Dagon their god, and to rejoice, for they said, "Our god has given Samson our enemy into our hands." When the people saw him, they praised their god, for they said, "Our god has given our enemy into our hands, Even the destroyer of our country, Who has slain many of us." It so happened when they were in high spirits, that they said, "Call for Samson, that he may amuse us." So they called for Samson from the prison, and he entertained them." (Judges 16:22-25)

It's pitiful to see Samson as a figure of fun here. He who was meant to provide deliverance for Israel; now provided entertainment for the Philistines. In the Psalms, it says of the

Lord Jesus that he became the song of the drunkards, the talk of those who sat in the gate, a topic of mirth, but his death would change all that. And Samson's about to die too – but let's not run ahead. We'll rejoin Judges chapter 16:

> "And they made [Samson] stand between the pillars. Then Samson said to the boy who was holding his hand, "Let me feel the pillars on which the house rests, that I may lean against them." Now the house was full of men and women, and all the lords of the Philistines were there. And about 3,000 men and women were on the roof looking on while Samson was amusing them. Then Samson called to the LORD and said, "O Lord GOD, please remember me and please strengthen me just this time, O God, that I may at once be avenged of the Philistines for my two eyes."
>
> Samson grasped the two middle pillars on which the house rested, and braced himself against them, the one with his right hand and the other with his left. And Samson said, "Let me die with the Philistines!" And he bent with all his might so that the house fell on the lords and all the people who were in it. So the dead whom he killed at his death were more than those whom he killed in his life. Then his brothers and all his father's household came down, took him, brought him up and buried him between Zorah and Eshtaol in the tomb of Manoah his father. Thus he had judged Israel twenty years." (Judges 16-26-31)

It's been said correctly that this was Samson's greatest exploit – that Samson's greatest victory was achieved in his death. For the Bible says: 'the dead whom he killed at his death were more than those whom he killed in his life.' It's certainly true of the Lord Jesus that his greatest victory was achieved through his death. How great was the victory he accomplished through his death on the cross! It was 'through death' that he rendered 'powerless him who had the power of death, that is, the devil' (Hebrews 2:14). During his ministry, the Lord had asked: "how can anyone enter the strong man's house and carry off his property, unless he first binds the strong man? And then he will plunder his house" (Matthew 12:29)

It was at the cross, through death, that the Lord bound Satan and plundered his domain: "For He rescued us from the domain of darkness, and transferred us to the kingdom of His beloved Son, in whom we have redemption, the forgiveness of sins" (Colossians 1:13-14). And it's an eternal redemption, for 'by one offering He has perfected for all time those who are sanctified' (Hebrews 10:14). Yes, the Lord's enemy was defeated at the cross, and in acknowledgement of that every power in heaven and earth must fall down before him (Philippians 2:10)! Samson brought the temple of Dagon crashing to the ground, but at the cross the entire bulwark of Satan's kingdom and dark domain was, in effect, brought crashing down, as the prince of this world was cast out.

Praise God there's such power in the blood – the blood of Christ, his Son. No wonder we sing 'There's power in the blood'! What wonders have resulted from the cross of Jesus! Let's review just some of them together, for I can't think of a better way with which to bring our current series to a conclusion, than to focus on the cross – and on all that it was designed to bring to us.

As believers, we're tasting the power of Christ's victory in many different ways even now. The apostle Paul begins his letter to the churches of God in Galatia with these words: "Grace to you and peace from God our Father and the Lord Jesus Christ, who gave Himself for our sins so that He might rescue us from this present evil age. (Galatians 1:3-4). This is not about taking us out of the world; it's to do with taking the world out of us. This is not some future deliverance, but a present, day-to-day deliverance – and notice how it's included in the purpose for which Christ died. God saves us and leaves us in the world for a purpose: to live the remainder of our lives for him, and not for ourselves – as Second Corinthians chapter 5 shows:

> "For the love of Christ controls us, having concluded this, that one died for all ... so that they who live might no longer live for themselves, but for Him who died and rose again on their behalf." (2 Corinthians 5:15)

And the purposes of God in and through the death of Christ are by no means limited to us as individuals – far from it. Paul writing to Titus talks about "the blessed hope and the appearing of the glory of our great God and Savior, Christ Jesus, who gave Himself for us to redeem us from every lawless deed, and to purify for Himself a people for His own possession, zealous for good deeds" (Titus 2:13-14). In the death of Christ, God had a people in view. There was even an unbelieving high priest in

Israel, who, though he was unbelieving, nevertheless prophesied that Jesus was going to die for the nation, "and not for the nation only, but in order that He might also gather together into one the children of God who are scattered abroad" (John 11:52).

So, a major part of God's purpose through the death of Christ was to gather believers together, so that they'd be united in their service for him in this world. So important was this to the Lord Jesus that it dominated the thoughts he expressed in prayer just hours before his death on the cross. We find those thoughts recorded in John's Gospel, chapter 17, where Jesus prays:

> "But now I come to You; and these things I speak in the world so that they may have My joy made full in themselves. I have given them Your word; and the world has hated them, because they are not of the world, even as I am not of the world. I do not ask You to take them out of the world, but to keep them from the evil one. They are not of the world, even as I am not of the world. Sanctify them in the truth; Your word is truth.

> As You sent Me into the world, I also have sent them into the world. For their sakes I sanctify Myself, that they themselves also may be sanctified in truth. I do not ask on behalf of these alone, but for those also who believe in Me through their word; that they may all be one; even as You, Father, are in Me and I in You, that they also may be in Us, so that the world may

believe that You sent Me. The glory which You have given Me I have given to them, that they may be one, just as We are one; (John 17:13-22).

This is a staggering prayer of the Lord Jesus on the eve of his cross experience. In it, he requests that we may be as closely related to the Father and the Son as they are to each other! That we might be as closely bound together in unity to the Father and the Son, as the Father and Son are to each other. Jesus envisages the loving relationship which binds the Father and the Son together in the mystery of the eternal Trinity being reflected in our own loving relationship with God and with each other as the people of God. How is this quality of unity possible? Only the wonder of Christ's death could accomplish that! What a victory it was! What wonders it's made possible!

This was the motivation for Paul going around as recorded in Acts 14:22, appointing elders in newly planted churches of God, urging them to continue in the Faith as they entered into this experience of being wonderfully unified as the people of God in God's kingdom on his earth.

And so, quite fittingly, it's with an enhanced appreciation of our Saviour's work at the cross – and the scale of its victory - that our study on Samson now comes to an end. Samson, who also recorded his greatest victory in his death. Overall, I hope we've enjoyed seeing some thought-provoking parallels between the life of Samson and the life of Christ. Samson's own life providing a very flawed picture of the perfection of the Lord Jesus as the ultimate Saviour.

SEARCH FOR TRUTH RADIO BROADCASTS

───

S earch for Truth Radio has been a ministry of the Churches of God (see www.churchesofgod.info) since 1978. Free Search for Truth podcasts can be listened to online or downloaded at four locations:

At SFT's own dedicated podcast site: www.searchfortruth.podbean.com

Via Itunes using the podcast app (search for Search For Truth)

On the Churches of God website: https://churchesofgod.info/media/#_Radio

On the Transworld Radio website: (http://www.twr360.org/programs/ministry_id,103)

Alternatively, see below for details of digital and analogue radio timings.

Europe Listen online at www.twr.org.uk/live.htm[1] or SKY Digital Channel 0138 (11.390 GHz, ID 53555) and Freesat channel 790 and Freeview 733 in the UK - Saturday at 07.30 and Sunday at 06.45.

Malawi - Sunday on TWR Malawi FM Network at 06.45 UTC+2 (89.1 - 106.5 FM)

───

1. http://www.twr.org.uk/live.htm

South East Asia - On Reach Beyond – Australia on Mondays 13.15 UTC, 25m band SW (15540 kHz.)

India - Tuesday and Friday on TWR Guam at 15.15, 19m band SW (12120 kHz.)

Thailand - Wednesday on TWR Guam at 08.50, 19m band SW (11965 kHz.)

CONTACTING SEARCH FOR TRUTH

———

If you have enjoyed reading one of our books or listening to a radio broadcast, we would love to know about that, or answer any questions that you might have.

Contact us at:

SFT c/o Hayes, Press, The Barn, Flaxlands, Wootton Bassett, Swindon, Wiltshire SN4 8DY

P.O. Box 748, Ringwood, Victoria 3134, Australia

P.O.Box 70115, Chilomoni, Blantyre, Malawi

Web site: www.searchfortruth.org.uk

Email: sft@churchesofgod.info

Also, if you have enjoyed reading this book and/or others in the series, we would really appreciate it if you could just take a couple of minutes to leave a brief review where you downloaded the book - it really is a very good way of spreading the word about our ministry.

Thanks and God bless!

Did you love *Samson: A Type of Christ*? Then you should read *Abraham: Friend of God*[1] by Brian Johnston!

Bible teacher, missionary and radio broadcaster, Brian Johnston's conversational and down to earth approach provides an informative biography and commentary of one of the most important characters in the Old Testament of our Bibles – Abraham the nomad. Abraham was known for his great example of faith and for being a "Friend of God", but his life was far from plain sailing. Brian draws out a number of lessons for our discipleship today in this helpful Bible study.

---

1. https://books2read.com/u/m2oxpr

2. https://books2read.com/u/m2oxpr

Also by Brian Johnston

Healthy Churches - God's Bible Blueprint For Growth
Hope for Humanity: God's Fix for a Broken World
First Corinthians: Nothing But Christ Crucified
Bible Answers to Listeners' Questions
Living in God's House: His Design in Action
Christianity 101: Seven Bible Basics
Nights of Old: Bible Stories of God at Work
Daniel Decoded: Deciphering Bible Prophecy
A Test of Commitment: 15 Challenges to Stimulate Your
Devotion to Christ
John's Epistles - Certainty in the Face of Change
If Atheism Is True...
8 Amazing Privileges of God's People: A Bible Study of Romans
9:4-5
Learning from Bible Grandparents
Increasing Your Christian Footprint
Christ-centred Faith
Mindfulness That Jesus Endorses
Amazing Grace! Paul's Gospel Message to the Galatians
Abraham: Friend of God
The Future in Bible Prophecy
Unlocking Hebrews
Learning How To Pray - From the Lord's Prayer

About the Bush: The Five Excuses of Moses
The Five Loves of God
Deepening Our Relationship With Christ
Really Good News For Today!
A Legacy of Kings - Israel's Chequered History
Minor Prophets: Major Issues!
The Tabernacle - God's House of Shadows
Tribes and Tribulations - Israel's Predicted Personalities
Once Saved, Always Saved - The Reality of Eternal Security
After God's Own Heart : The Life of David
Jesus: What Does the Bible Really Say?
God: His Glory, His Building, His Son
The Feasts of Jehovah in One Hour
Knowing God - Reflections on Psalm 23
Praying with Paul
Get Real ... Living Every Day as an Authentic Follower of
Christ
A Crisis of Identity
Double Vision: Hidden Meanings in the Prophecy of Isaiah
Samson: A Type of Christ
Great Spiritual Movements
Take Your Mark's Gospel
Total Conviction - 4 Things God Wants You To Be Fully
Convinced About
Esther: A Date With Destiny
Experiencing God in Ephesians
The Book of James - Epistle of Straw?
The Supremacy of Christ
The Visions of Zechariah
Encounters at the Cross
Five Sacred Solos - The Truths That the Reformation Recovered

Kingdom of God: Past, Present or Future?
Overcoming Objections to Christian Faith
Stronger Than the Storm - The Last Words of Jesus
Fencepost Turtles - People Placed by God
Five Woman and a Baby - The Genealogy of Jesus
Pure Milk - Nurturing New Life in Jesus
Jesus: Son Over God's House
Salt and the Sacrifice of Christ
The Glory of God
The Way: Being a New Testament Disciple
Power Outage - Christianity Unplugged
Home Truths
60 Minutes to Raise the Dead

About the Author

Born and educated in Scotland, Brian worked as a government scientist until God called him into full-time Christian ministry on behalf of the Churches of God (www.churchesofgod.info). His voice has been heard on Search For Truth radio broadcasts for over 30 years (visit www.searchfortruth.podbean.com) during which time he has been an itinerant Bible teacher throughout the UK and Canada. His evangelical and missionary work outside the UK is primarily in Belgium and The Philippines. He is married to Rosemary, with a son and daughter.

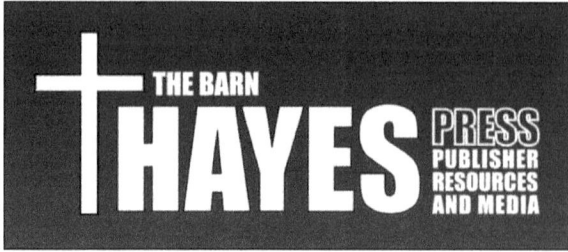

About the Publisher

Hayes Press (www.hayespress.org) is a registered charity in the United Kingdom, whose primary mission is to disseminate the Word of God, mainly through literature. It is one of the largest distributors of gospel tracts and leaflets in the United Kingdom, with over 100 titles and hundreds of thousands despatched annually. In addition to paperbacks and eBooks, Hayes Press also publishes Plus Eagles Wings, a fun and educational Bible magazine for children, and Golden Bells, a popular daily Bible reading calendar in wall or desk formats. Also available are over 100 Bibles in many different versions, shapes and sizes, Bible text posters and much more!

www.ingramcontent.com/pod-product-compliance
Lightning Source LLC
Chambersburg PA
CBHW060703030426
42337CB00017B/2743